Tudor and Stuart Times

Jane Shuter

Adam Hook

Judith Maguire

HEINEMANN
EDUCATIONAL

CONTENTS

Heinemann Educational
a division of Heinemann Educational Books Ltd
Halley Court, Jordan Hill, Oxford OX2 8EJ

OXFORD LONDON EDINBURGH MADRID
ATHENS BOLOGNA PARIS MELBOURNE
SYDNEY AUCKLAND SINGAPORE TOKYO
IBADAN NAIROBI HARARE GABORONE
PORTSMOUTH NH (USA)

First published 1992

**British Library Cataloguing in Publication
Data** is available from the British Library on
request.

ISBN 0 435 31800 4

Designed by Ron Kamen, Green Door Design
Ltd, Basingstoke, Hants

Printed in Spain by Mateu Cromo

Acknowledgements
The authors and publisher would like to thank
the following for permission to reproduce
photographs:

Bodleian Library: 4H, 5L, 7F
Bridgeman Art Library/
    Belvoir Castle, Leicestershire: p.4 (*Henry VIII*)
    Bristol Museum and Art Gallery: 3B
    Christie's London: p.4 (*Henry VII*)
    Private Collection: p.4 (*Elizabeth I*)
    Society of Antiquaries, London: p.4 (*Mary I*)
    Roy Miles Gallery: p.5 (*James I*)
    Victoria & Albert Museum: p.5 (*James II*)
    Trustees of the Weston Park Foundation: p.5
    (*Charles I*)
British Film Institute: 11G
British Library: 3C, 8F, 14K

Viscount Coke and the Trustees of the Holkham
Estate: 5I
Devonshire Collection, Chatsworth. Reproduced
by permission of the Chatsworth Settlement
Trustees: 6A
Library of Congress, Washington D.C: 10D
C.M. Dixon: 11D
By permission of the Folger Shakespeare
Library: 3I
Freer Gallery of Art, Smithsonian Institution,
Washington D.C: 7J
Fotomas Index/Marquess of Salisbury: 2A
Trustees of the Geffrye Museum: 4D
Michael Holford/British Museum: 3A
Hulton-Deutsch Collection: 4A, 6J
Mansell Collection: 10C, 13D, 13H
Museum of London: 7D, 14A, 14E
National Maritime Museum, London: 7G, 9A,
9C, 9F
National Portrait Gallery: 3D, 6C, p.4 (*Edward
VI*), p.5 (*Charles II*), p.5 (*Mary II, William III* and
Queen Anne)
National Trust Photographic Library/John
Bethall: 5E
New College, Oxford/Philip Parkhouse: 10F
Pepys Library, Magdalene College, Cambridge:
12A
Royal Collection, St James's Palace © Her
Majesty the Queen: 7C
Society of Antiquaries of London: 3F
Jamie Stamp: 2B
Victoria & Albert Museum: 7I
Bob Watkins: 2C
Weidenfeld & Nicolson Archives: 3G

Cover photograph shows Baron Cobham and
his family. Reproduced by permission of the
Marquess of Bath.

Our thanks to Mike Mullet of the University of
Lancaster for his comments in the preparation
of this book.

HENRY VII m. Elizabeth of York
(1485–1509)

Arthur
(died)

HENRY VIII m. 1. Catharine   2. Ann Boleyn   3. Jane Seymour
(1509–1547)   of Aragon

EDWARD VI
(1547–1553)

MARY I
(1553–1558)

ELIZABETH I
(1558–1603)

Key

m. =   married

(1509–1547) =   years as king
                  or queen

————   Tudors

————   Stuarts

Activities

1 Make a list of all the Tudor **monarchs** (kings and queens) with the dates they ruled. Make sure you write them down in the order they ruled.

2 Make a list of all the Stuart monarchs (kings and queens) with the dates they ruled.

3 How many years was there no monarch, between Charles I and Charles II?

1 Who were the Tudors and Stuarts?

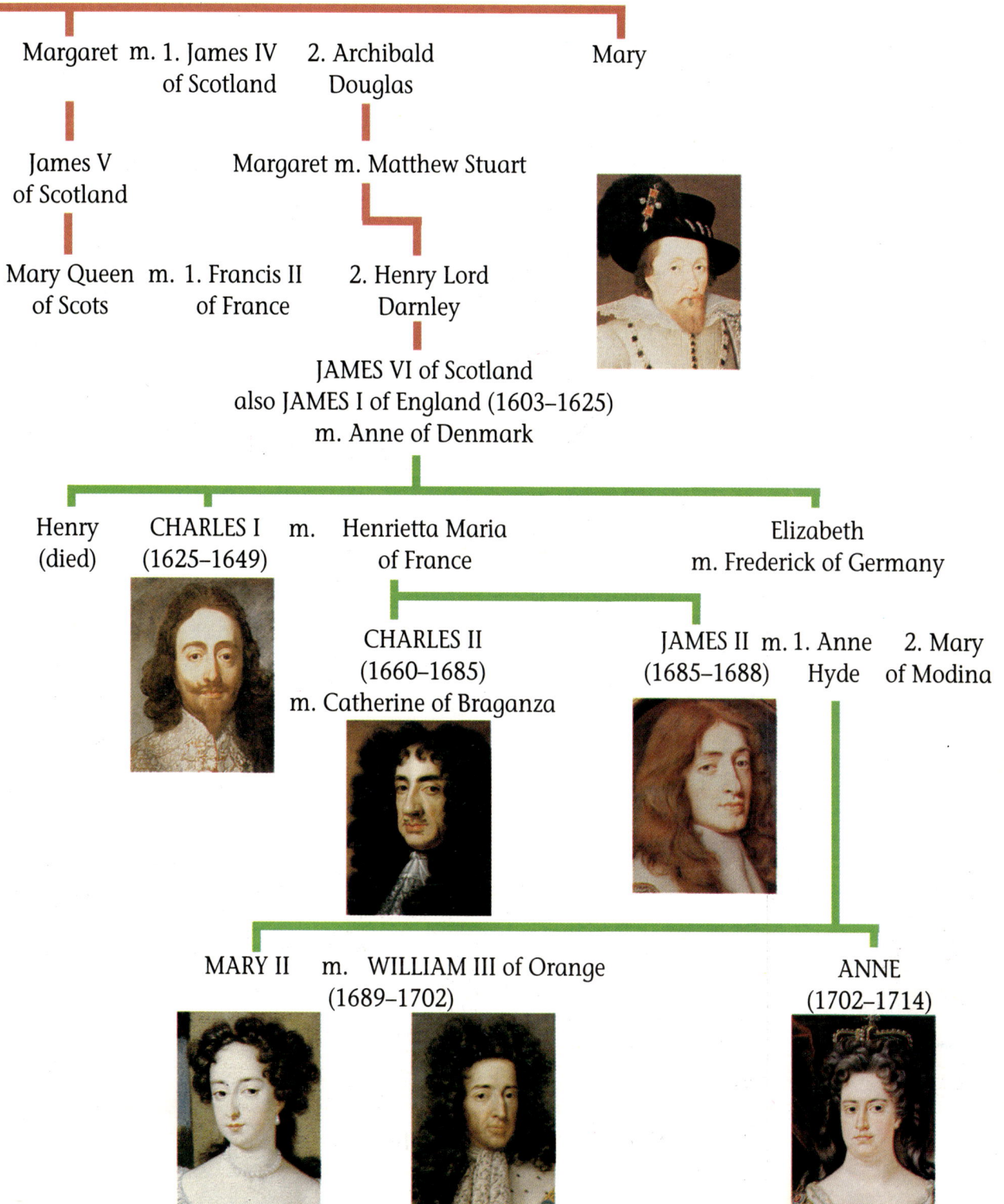

Margaret m. 1. James IV   2. Archibald   Mary
            of Scotland   Douglas

James V   Margaret m. Matthew Stuart
of Scotland

Mary Queen   m. 1. Francis II   2. Henry Lord
of Scots   of France   Darnley

JAMES VI of Scotland
also JAMES I of England (1603–1625)
m. Anne of Denmark

Henry   CHARLES I   m.   Henrietta Maria   Elizabeth
(died)   (1625–1649)   of France   m. Frederick of Germany

CHARLES II   JAMES II m. 1. Anne   2. Mary
(1660–1685)   (1685–1688)   Hyde   of Modina
m. Catherine of Braganza

MARY II   m.   WILLIAM III of Orange   ANNE
            (1689–1702)   (1702–1714)

2 Then and now

The Tudors and the Stuarts reigned for over 200 years. The last Stuart monarch, Queen Anne, died nearly 300 years ago. There are ways in which the people who lived in England then are very different from us today. But there are also ways in which they are the same.

Source A

A picture of a wedding in Bermondsey in about 1592.

A wedding in Bermondsey in 1992.

Bermondsey in 1992.

How have things changed?

1 Look at Sources A and C.
   a How is Bermondsey different between 1592 and 1992?
   b How is Bermondsey the same between 1592 and 1992?

2 Look at Sources A and B.
   a How are weddings different between 1592 and 1992?
   b How are weddings the same between 1592 and 1992?
   c Do you think all weddings in 1992 looked like Source B?
   d Do you think all weddings in 1592 looked like Source A?

3 How religion changed

In 1485 England was a Catholic country. Everyone went to church on Sunday. They all heard the same service, in Latin. Most of them would not have understood the service.

In 1530 Henry VIII was king. He wanted to have a son to be king after him. His first wife had many babies. But only one girl lived. Henry wanted to end his marriage and marry again. Catholics could not do this easily. Only the **Pope**, as Head of the Catholic Church, could give permission to end a marriage. Henry asked the Pope to do this. The Pope said no. So Henry made himself Head of the English Church, instead of the Pope, and got a **divorce**.

Parliament agreed to the change. Some people agreed because they wanted Henry to marry again. Some agreed because they thought the Catholic Church was too powerful and rich. These people wanted to **reform** the Church, to make the people in it think more about God, and less about power and money.

Henry started the **reformation** of the Church. He inspected the abbeys, whose monks and nuns were said to be very rich and not very religious. He closed the abbeys down, and took their money for himself.

Source A

Many of the monks go hunting and shooting. The prior is often drunk.

The abbess cannot read, nor can any of her women.

The prior likes to play dice, and spends a lot of money on this.

Three of the reports from the people who inspected the abbeys.

Source B

This painting shows the closing down of Syon Abbey in 1539. It was painted about 300 years after it happened.

8

This picture of a monk drinking wine comes from a decorated book. Monks had been accused of drunkenness for centuries.

Activities

1 Read Source A. Look at Source C. Do they have the same sort of view of monks and nuns?

2 Reports like those in Source A were from people sent to find out what was **wrong** with the abbeys. Would this make a difference to what they said?

3 Look at Source B. Read the caption.
   a What view does this give of the monks and nuns?
   b Is this view the same as the other sources?

4 a What reason for closing the abbeys would you give if you only had Source A?
   b What reason for closing the abbeys would you give if you only had Source B?
   c You have both sources. What do you say now?

The **Reformation** made people think about how they really wanted to worship. **Catholics** wanted to worship in the same way they always had. **Protestants** wanted to go back to the way people worshipped in the Bible. But they could not agree about how this should be done. So there were many different sorts of Protestantism. Some Protestants thought that people should worship God very simply. They were called **Puritans**. The **official** religion (the one the government wanted people to use) kept changing.

Source D

1547–1553: Edward VI was a Protestant and wanted everyone else to be Protestant too. He had the first Prayer Book in English made. He stopped all Catholic services. The soldiers in this picture are pulling down Catholic statues.

Catholics and Protestants

Catholics wanted:
- The Pope as Head of the Church.
- Services in Latin.
- Lots of statues, ornament and paintings in churches.

Most Protestants wanted:
- No Pope.
- Services in English.
- Plain churches.

Source E

1553–1558: Mary was a Catholic. She wanted to make sure that everyone in the country became Catholic. This picture shows Protestants being burned for not becoming Catholics in the reign of Queen Mary I.

1625–1714: England stayed a Protestant country. After the Civil War (when there was no king or queen) the government was very Protestant. It even banned Christmas! There were worries about Catholic plots all through the period. But by the time of Queen Anne people were sure enough that England would stay Protestant to make fans like this one to celebrate.

Source
F

1558–1625: Elizabeth I was a Protestant, so she changed the Catholic ways brought in by her sister, Mary I. But she did not want to force everyone to have one religion. As long as people went to church, or open-air services like the one in the picture, she did not worry about how they worshipped in their own homes. Things settled down and carried on in the same way into the reign of James I.

Activitiy

1 **a** Copy the list of kings and queens below. Use the family tree at the front of the book to add the dates they ruled.

- *Henry VIII*
- *Edward VI*
- *Mary I*
- *Elizabeth I*
- *James I*
- *Queen Anne*

b Now add to your list the religion that was the official religion when they reigned.

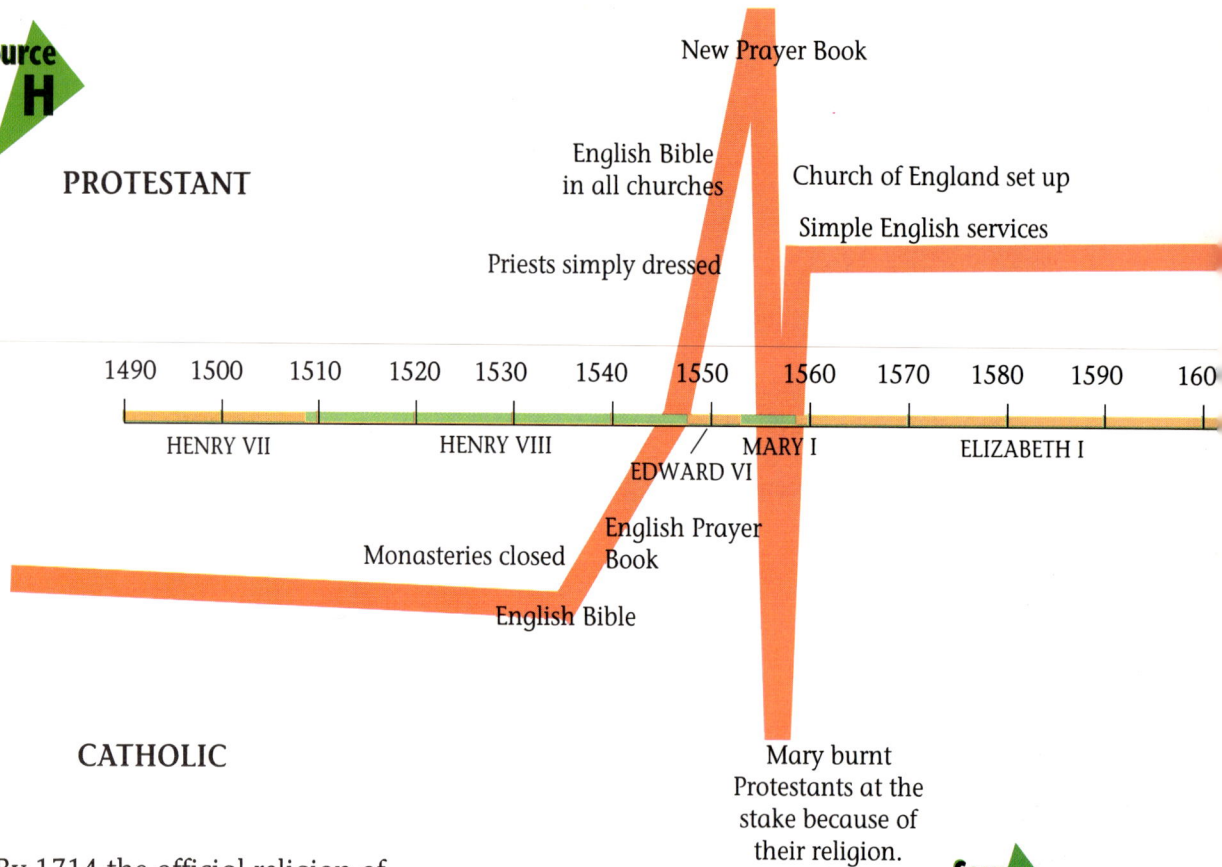

PROTESTANT

New Prayer Book

English Bible
in all churches

Church of England set up

Simple English services

Priests simply dressed

| 1490 | 1500 | 1510 | 1520 | 1530 | 1540 | 1550 | 1560 | 1570 | 1580 | 1590 | 160 |

HENRY VII

HENRY VIII

MARY I

EDWARD VI

ELIZABETH I

English Prayer
Book

Monasteries closed

English Bible

CATHOLIC

Mary burnt
Protestants at the
stake because of
their religion.

By 1714 the official religion of Britain had changed many times. Services were now in English, and people could follow them in their Bible and Prayer Book. But, despite all the changes, some things were the same. Almost everyone still believed in God. They were still Christians. They still went to church on Sunday. They still marked the important days in their lives (like births, weddings and deaths) with church services.

Activity

Look at Source H. What idea do you think this picture was trying to give to the people who came to church?

How did things change?

1 **a** Write down two ways in which religion changed between 1485 and 1714.
   b Write down two ways in which it stayed the same.

2 Look at Source H.
   a When were the religious changes most **rapid** (quickest)?
   b When were the religious changes most **gradual** (slowest)?

Christmas back

Christmas was
banned

Back to very
plain services

mes Bible

| 0 | 1620 | 1630 | 1640 | 1650 | 1660 | 1670 | 1680 | 1690 | 1700 | 1710 | 1714 |

S I   CHARLES I   No King or   CHARLES II   JAMES II   ANNE
                               Queen   WILLIAM
                                                                and MARY

Catholic wife, had always
been Catholic

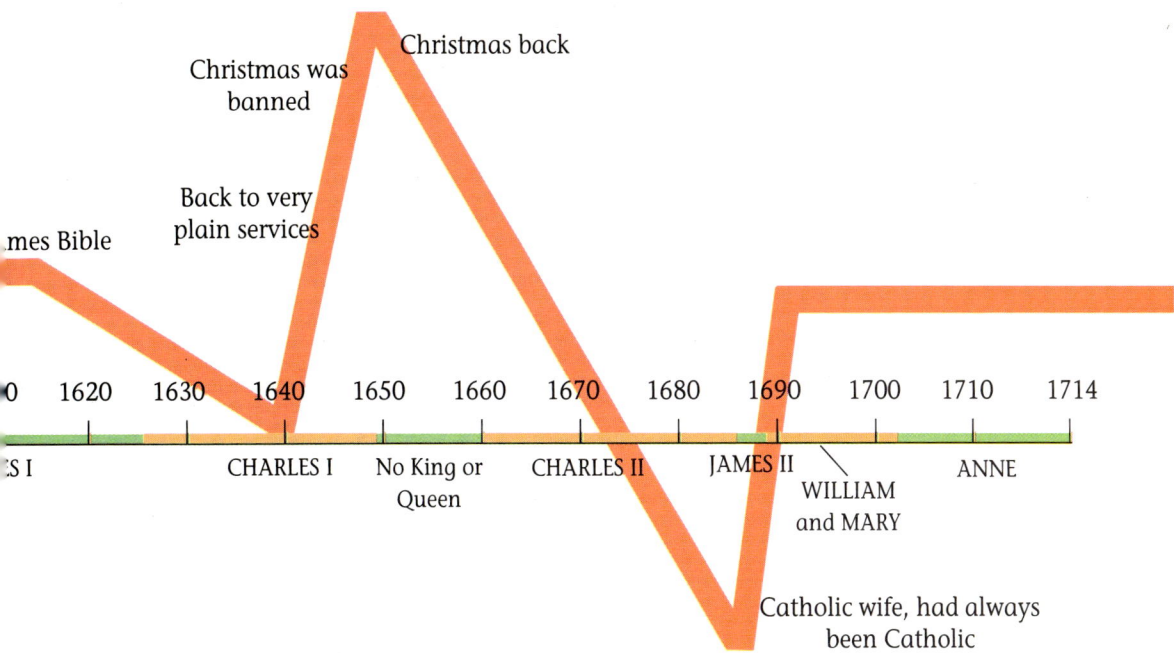

▼ A painting on a church wall, from about 1500. It shows
the Last Judgement when people were sent either to
heaven or to hell. Pictures were used to show the most
important ideas from the Bible, as the services were in
Latin which most people could not understand.

4 What was town life like?

From 1485 to 1714 towns changed a lot. They got bigger, especially London. We will look at town life in the time of Queen Elizabeth I.

Towns were busy and exciting. They had markets, barbers, entertainments, shops and even schools. There was a lot to see and do. But towns did not have drains, rubbish collections, tap water or street lights. They were noisy, crowded and smelly.

Many poor people came to the towns to look for work. Often they did not find any. So they had to beg or steal to keep alive.

There was no tap water. People had to fetch their own water, or buy it from a water seller like the man in this picture. Often the water was taken straight from the river. People also threw their rubbish in the river.

Town Councils tried to look after the streets, but mostly failed. Some main streets were cleaned and some were paved, but most streets were just like open sewers.

Written by a modern historian.

Activities

1 Read Source B. Look at Source C. What is the same?

2 Look at the shop sign. The sign is a picture because most people could not read. What is the shop selling?

3 Draw a shop sign for: a fishmonger, a shoemaker and a butcher.

4 Look at Source A and read the caption. What do you think the water was like? Why did people still buy it?

A modern artist's idea of what an Elizabethan street looked like. The shops looked on to the street. Each shop had a big window shutter which folded down to make a counter.

Rich people lived in large houses, with many rooms. They spent their time eating, drinking, going shopping, or amusing themselves.

Most of the other people in the town had to work. **Craftworkers** lived and worked in the same building. The ground floor of the house was the workshop and shop. Everyone in the town with the same trade had to join a **guild**. So shoemakers would have had a guild of their own, which they paid to join. Members of the guilds would each have an **apprentice**. The apprentice lived with the family to learn the trade.

Source D

A typical Elizabethan room, from a modern museum.

Most houses are wooden. Roofs are tiled or thatched. Floors are made of stone or plaster. The walls are plastered and painted or covered with cloths or tapestries. Rich people now have stoves. Glass is used more for windows, not polished horn or woven reeds. Houses have more chimneys, more rooms and more furniture.

Written in 1577 by William Harrison. He wrote a book about England at this time.

Poorer people eat chicken, milk, butter and cheese. The rich eat beef, venison, game birds and fish. They eat all they want. There is always something left and the servants eat that. If there is any left after this it is given to the poor. Rich people eat from silver or pewter, not wood. They drink from silver, pewter or glass.

Written by William Harrison in 1557.

People once ate breakfast, lunch at noon, dinner at five and supper before they went to bed. Now most people miss breakfast, eat dinner at eleven in the morning and supper at five. The poor eat what and when they can.

Written by William Harrison 1557.

Activities

Look closely at Source C on page 15. Then read Source E.

1 Make a list of everything mentioned in Source E that you can see in Source C.

2 a Draw the inside of a rich Elizabethan home showing food, people eating, the walls and a window.

  b What would you like to know to make your drawing more accurate?

Beggers all.

There are poor people everywhere. The rich should look after them. There are three sorts of poor: those who are poor because of a disaster, those who are poor because they cannot work and those who are poor because they will not work.

Written by William Harrison in 1557.

We should stop the building of houses in London for renting out. Many people are crowded into them. Up to twenty people have been found living in one room. These buildings are also badly built and cared for.

A letter written in 1590 to the Privy Council, who advised Elizabeth 1.

The poor and the law

Some town Councils had their own plans to help the poor. This was because the problem was worse in the towns. The Councils asked for money from people who were able to pay. This was then given to the poor.

Government laws about the poor saw them as three types, like those in Source I. It took the government a long time to see that some fit people were not working because they could not find work. At first the government punished fit people who were not working. Later they changed the law to try to give them work.

▲ Some beggars, drawn at the time.

Were things different then?

1 Look at Source C on page 15. Design a poster to show how busy Elizabethan towns were. Label the different types of people and the jobs they are doing.

2 Write a short description of your life in a Tudor town as:
a rich person;
a tradesman;
a poor person.

3 Look at Source H. Are all of these people beggars? How do you know?

4 Look at Source I and the information box about the poor and the law.
a What were the three types of beggars?
b Did the government change the way they treated any of them?

5 Elizabethan country life

Most towns got bigger in Elizabethan times. Even so, most people still lived in the countryside.

Most villages had at least one blacksmith, brewer and baker. Each village had a church, or was close to one. People grew enough food to feed the village. If they grew more food or made more things than they needed, or needed things they could not make, they went to the nearest market town to trade.

Source B

The people in the village needed each other. This does not mean they always got on. They got drunk, fought, argued over land, sometimes stole from each other. From time to time they even killed each other. The poor poached from the rich, the rich worked the poor too hard.

From a modern book about the village of Terling in Tudor and Stuart times.

Source A

A modern artist's idea of what an Elizabethan village looked like.

Source C

Most people had more than one job. They worked in the fields and then made extra money from any other skill that they had. So Matthew Mitchell of Terling was a labourer, brewer and tailor.

From a modern book about the village of Terling in Tudor and Stuart times.

Source D

People in Terling grew wheat, kept animals and had orchards and gardens. They could feed themselves on their own grain, meat, milk, butter and cheese.

From a modern book about the village of Terling in Tudor and Stuart times.

Activities

1 a Look at Source A. What work can you see going on?
  b Are any of these jobs not listed in the text?
  c Are any of the jobs in the text not shown in the picture? If so, what is the reason we cannot see them?

2 Read Source D.
  Imagine you were a villager with:
      land to grow wheat
      1 cow, 2 pigs, 4 sheep
      some chickens
      a share in an orchard.

  a What food would these give you?
  b What things other than food would these give you?

Life in the countryside was changing. People had farmed by dividing the fields into **strips.** The strips were farmed by different people. This meant that everyone got strips of good and bad land. By Elizabeth I's time some people were joining the strips together and making separate fields. They **enclosed** (fenced off) these fields. This was not the only change. Many big land owners changed from growing corn to keeping sheep. They got more money for wool than for corn. They also needed fewer workers, so had to pay less in wages.

Source E

An Elizabethan shepherd.

Source F

Sheep have eaten up our Meadows and our downs, Our corn, our wood, whole Villages and towns.

From one of many songs about the change to sheep farming made up at the time.

Source G

In the time of Queen Elizabeth I the population of England grew. So did the population of the village of Terling. No one was forced to leave the village because of enclosure or sheep farming. But a lot of people still had to leave just to find work.

From a modern book about the village of Terling in Tudor and Stuart times.

Source H

In a village which once had over a hundred people there are now only a shepherd and his sheep. The villagers have no homes. They go looking for work. The same is happening everywhere. They can find no work. So they beg. Some steal, and are hanged for it.

From a letter written to King Henry VIII. The letter was against enclosing fields and changing from wheat to sheep farming.

A picture showing a variety of farming jobs in Tudor times.

Activities

1 **a** How many people are working in Source I?
   b How many people are working in Source E?
   c What does Source H say has happened to all of the other people?
   d Is there a source that **agrees** with Source H? If so, which one?
   e Is there a source that **disagrees** with Source H? If so, which one?

2 Can you tell if Source H is right?

Most village houses in 1485 had one floor, with one or two rooms. They were made from the cheapest local building materials. They had no chimney, or kitchen. The windows were holes that could be covered by wooden shutters.

The villagers had very few things. Wills show that a mattress, some clothing and bedding, a folding table, a bench or stools and a few wooden or leather dishes were all that most people had.

Written by a modern historian.

Wills from about 1597 show that beds were becoming more common for ordinary people. Bedding and clothes were important enough to be listed in wills, and given to particular people. Most families had a chest or two to store things in. At this time people were beginning to use 'proper' tables and chairs, rather than folding tables and benches. Perhaps this was because they had more space.

From a modern book about the village of Terling in Tudor and Stuart times.

Ploughing before Tudor times.

A map made in 1597 shows that most of the houses were just one storey, often just one room. There was sometimes a room added to one end of the house. Most houses had chimneys to take the smoke away.

From a modern book about the village of Terling in Tudor and Stuart times.

How did things change?

1 Design a poster showing Elizabethan life in the countryside. Label the people and the jobs they are doing.

2 Look at Sources I and L.
   a How had ploughing methods changed?
   b Does this mean that all farming had changed slowly?

3 Compare Sources J, K and M.
   a List the things that are different between 1485 and 1597.
   b Which of Sources J and M best describes the farmhouse on the right of Source I? Explain your answer.

4 Read Sources J and K. How did life get better?

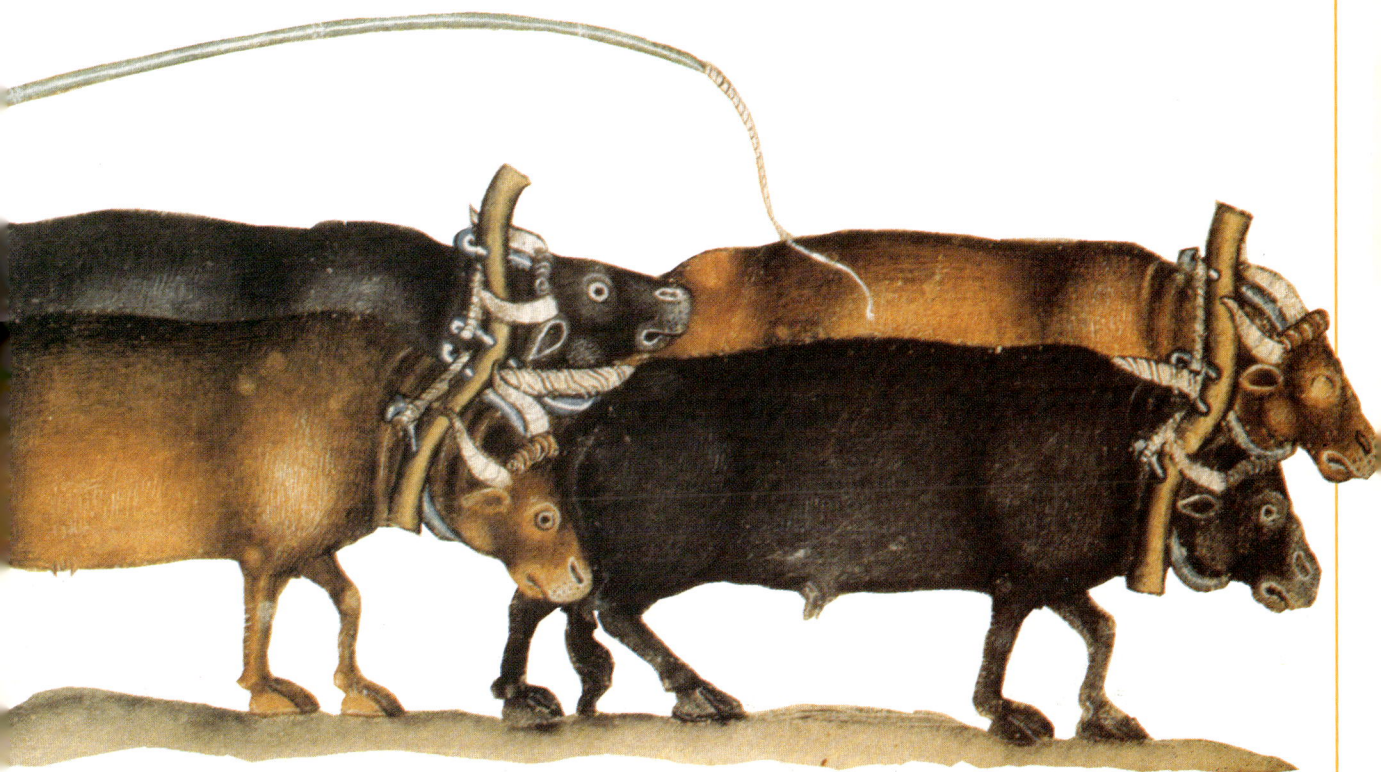

6 Entertainment in Shakespeare's time

How did people enjoy themselves in Shakespeare's time? Shakespeare was a famous playwright. He wrote most of his plays during the reign of James I. How people enjoyed themselves then depended on who they were, and where they lived.

The King and the people who lived with him, his **Court**, spent a lot of money on entertainment. **Masques** were written for them (masques were like modern musicals). Often they acted the parts themselves. They wore expensive costumes and make-up. There were also huge feasts and dances.

Towns had many shows, especially London, which had several theatres. Towns with no theatres used the yard of the biggest inn. Theatres were used for plays, and also by magicians and acrobats. At home, people liked to play cards, chess and draughts.

Source A

This is a costume for a masque by a famous designer called Inigo Jones. He also designed buildings for James I.

A masque in a country house in about 1610.

From a picture painted for Sir Henry Unton in 1596.

Activities

1 Look at Source A and read the caption. Do you think this costume is for a masque at the King's Court, or not?

2 Look at Source B and read the caption. Do you think this masque is at Court or not?

3 Look at Source C.
   a Can you find a masque here? If so, what colour are the actors wearing?
   b Make a list of all the other amusements you can find.

A modern artist's idea of what a play in a London theatre
would have looked like at the time of King James I.

E If you stand below you only pay a penny. If you want to sit in the comfortable seats it costs another penny. During the performance food and drink are taken around the audience.

Written in 1599 by Thomas Platter in his book *Travels in England*.

F I was at a theatre in Venice and saw a comedy acted. The theatre was not as grand as ours. The actors were not as well dressed as ours. The music was not as good as ours. I saw a woman act, a thing I never saw before.

Written in 1611 by Thomas Coryat in his book *Crudities*.

Scenery

There was a lot less scenery and fewer props than we have today. Lots of the scene setting came in what the actors were saying, to help the audience imagine the scene.

Here are some examples of this kind of scene setting:

"So this is the forest of Arden..."

"I see a rocky island..."

"The waves are high, the wind howls..."

"This bank is covered with flowers"

"What ugly hag is this..."

Activity

Read the information box about scenery. Write a short play to act out for other groups. You cannot use any props or costumes. You will need to think carefully about how people will know who you are, where you are, and what you are doing.

See if they can work out who you are, where you are, and what you are doing.

G

1	rock	1	globe
1	cage	1	sceptre
2	tombs	1	lion
2	coffins	2	lions' heads
1	bed	1	snake
1	helmet	4	crowns
8	lances	1	ghost's crown
3	clubs	10	sets of stockings
1	shield	16	jackets
1	wooden hatchet	17	dresses (4 have been lost)
1	leather hatchet	14	cloaks

A list of some of the props (equipment and costumes) of a London theatre.

In the country people had outdoor amusements. Rich people hunted or fished. Travelling actors came to their homes. People played football and practiced archery. There were yearly fairs and celebrations.

Source
H

King James produced a *Book of Sports* in 1618, which was read aloud after the Sunday church service. It said that Sunday entertainments after church were not wrong, as some people said. It said that people needed the exercise and change after working all week.

Written by a modern historian.

Source
I

Sometimes necks are broken, sometimes backs. Sometimes arms are put out of joint, or legs. Sometimes their noses run with blood. There are no rules that I can tell. The man with the ball must run with it for his life.

Philip Stubbes writing about football in 1583. He was a Puritan and felt that people thought too much about fun on Sundays, and not enough about God.

Source
J

The Cotswold Games – a yearly fair.

These are some games that children played at the time.

Were things different then?

1 Compare Source D with Source E.
   a What things are the same?
   b What things are different?

2 Look at Source A on page 6.
   List the different amusements you can see.

3 Look at Source J.
   a What sports can you see?
   b How many still go on today?

4 Look at Source K.
   a What games can you see?
   b How many still go on today?

7 How transport changed

The way that people travelled changed between 1485 and 1714. There were more types of transport in 1714, and more people were travelling. Coaches pulled by horses were used more and more. They were very uncomfortable on the bumpy roads, and had to be improved. In Stuart times there were many horse-drawn coach services, like our bus or train services today. People even wrote and published books showing the best routes around the country. Maps were more carefully drawn and became more accurate. But travelling was still difficult and, whether by sea or by land, dangerous.

Source C

Source D

Source A

In 1485 roads were bad. People either rode or walked. Carts were used if there was no other way to move something. They often got stuck in muddy or rutted roads.

Written by a modern historian.

Source B

Sir Christopher Wren mended the road near Whitehall in London. It had been badly kept and was muddy and full of holes. He dug down some two foot. Then he put layers of tar and earth down, until the road was level again. Now it is good. It only needs mending in bad weather and where the coaches have worn it out.

Written in 1696.

Different ways of travelling, from a painting made in 1520.

Activity

Copy this table. Fill in the different ways of travelling described in each source. Choose another picture source and fill in the last column.

Ways of travelling				
Source A	Source B	Source C	Source D	

Fish Street, London, in about 1700.

Ships changed more than any other form of transport. This was partly because ship design was important in wars. If ships were designed well, they won more battles. It was also because people travelled more by sea, over longer distances, to trade and explore.

People wanted to trade with other countries. They had travelled over land to trade with countries like India and China. But land routes were long and difficult. There were often wars, which stopped traders moving about. Sea routes would be easier. People also wanted to explore. They wanted to find new lands to trade with. They wanted to own these lands too.

Source E

21 April: I think I will build a coach house and a stable, and have a coach of my own. I can afford it. I am almost ashamed to be seen travelling in a hired coach.

24 April: I went by water at ten at night to the Swan Inn. I walked home from there at midnight.

Written in 1667 by Samuel Pepys, who lived in London.

Source F

Early traders in Venice, Italy, painted in about 1400. River travel was common in England too, especially in cities which had rivers running through them.

Trading ships in Bristol in the early 1700s.

Activities

1 Read Source E. How did Samuel Pepys travel around London?

2 Look at Sources F and G.
   a Write down four things about the ships that are the same.
   b Write down four things about the ships that are different.

3 Why do you think that people making long journeys further out to sea would want:
   a more sails
   b no oars?

Trade was important in Tudor and Stuart times. English people wanted **cloths**, like silk. They wanted **spices**, like cinnamon, pepper and cloves. They wanted sugar and lemons. In Stuart times people started to drink hot chocolate, coffee and tea. These things were not grown or made in England. People had to trade English things for them. People mostly traded wool for these goods.

Traders often made a lot of money. They charged very high prices for the goods they brought home. They took big risks. A whole cargo of spices or silks would be lost if a ship sank. The right to trade with foreign countries was so important that wars were fought over it. The English and Dutch fought three separate wars over trade in 1652, 1665 and 1672.

Source I

A cup made for holding spices from the Indies.

Source H

At the Change I heard two rich ships have come home, which were feared sunk. Sir Thomas Chamberlain showed me letters from the East Indies. They show how the Dutch behave. They are rude to all English, even the people at our only trading post there. They beat several men, and hung our flag under theirs. They say they will be masters of all the southern seas.

Written in 1664 by Samuel Pepys. The Change was the Royal Exchange, a building where most London trading went on.

Activities

1 What does Source I tell you about how important spices were?

2 Look at Source J. Which one is supposed to be King James I?

3 Read the last sentence of the text, and Source H.
   a When was Source H written?
   b What was just about to happen?
   c How do you think traders at the Royal Exchange felt that day?

This painting shows the Indian emperor, Jahangir, being given presents by European kings. One of them is supposed to be James I.

How did things change?

1 List three ways that transport changed between 1485 and 1714.

2 List three ways that transport did not change between 1485 and 1714.

3 List three ways that transport is different now.

4 List three ways that transport is the same now.

8 The privateers: heroes or pirates?

When Elizabeth I was Queen, many English seamen went
exploring. They found new places, and new things to trade.
Walter Raleigh brought back potatoes and tobacco from America.
He also tried to set up the first English settlement there. Francis
Drake made a voyage right around the world looking for new
places to trade with.

There were trade routes set up to China, India, Africa, Russia and
America.

The merchants brought back silk from China, spices from India,
slaves and spices from Africa, furs from Russia and gold and
pearls from America.

Source A

TYPVS ORBIS TERRARVM.

A map made in 1587. You can see Drake's route
around the world.

The seamen making these voyages also fought the Spanish. They called themselves **privateers**. This meant that although they were not in the navy, the government said they could attack enemy ships. Much of the treasure they brought home came from Spanish ships they sank, or Spanish towns they raided, not from trade. The English thought they were helping their country. The Spanish saw them as pirates. Can we tell who was right?

Source B

Many people became rich through trade. John Hawkins, one of the privateers, had trouble with his first trade voyage. He made nothing. On his second voyage, selling African slaves in America, he made a huge profit.

Written by a modern historian.

Source C

I have heard exactly what the English have been doing in America. They have sailed into the harbours and traded all their things. Some of this has been done in a friendly way. Sometimes they have used force, and stolen all they could, far more than their things were worth.

Written by a German trader, living in Spain at the time.

Drake's voyage around the world

Dec. 1577: Left Plymouth with five ships.

Oct. 1578: Reached Chile, in South America. Just one ship, the *Golden Hind*, left.

Dec. 1578: Captured Spanish gold.

July 1579: Claimed California for England.

Oct. 1579: Made trade treaty with Ternate (an island off the coast of Asia). Left with six tons of spice.

Feb. 1580 *Golden Hind* stuck on a sandbank. Spice thrown overboard to lose weight.

Sept.1580: Home to England with Spanish gold.

Activities

Read the information box about Drake's voyage, and follow his journey on the map.

1 Where had Drake got to when he was left with only one ship?

2 How long did the whole journey take?

3 What event would you use if you wanted to show that Drake went to find trade?

4 What event would you use if you wanted to show that Drake went to get treasure?

Source D

In 1494, the Pope said the New World (America) was to be divided between Spain and Portugal. He said no other country could settle there, or trade with the people. No one else could have their gold.

Written by a modern historian.

Source E

In 1562 John Hawkins made his first trading voyage. He bought African slaves and arranged with the Spanish to sell them in America. He bought pearls, sugar and gold. He sent them back to England by way of Seville. The Spanish took them. They did not reply to letters from Queen Elizabeth asking for them to be given back.

Written by a modern historian.

Source F

Source G

Englishmen have robbed our merchant ships. They have taken everything. We have lost a lot. We have sent letters to the Queen of England to complain. Nothing has happened.

Written from Spain to the Spanish Ambassador in England.

Source H

Francis Drake has returned from the Indies. He captured several of our towns. He brought back 140 cannons and ammunition for them, about £1,000 worth of pearls, over £70,000 worth of gold and silver, and some other stuff.

I cannot send news of when the English ships might set out on another raid. Ships are leaving all the ports all the time, and there is no way of knowing where they are going to. Our ships should travel in groups. Even if they had to pay armed ships to guard them it would be worth it.

Written in 1586 by a Spanish spy in England.

◄ **A drawing of Drake's raid on the Spanish town of Santiago in 1585.**

What do people say about the past?

1 Read Source D.
  a Why might the Spanish see Drake as a pirate? What source could they use to support this view?
  b Why would the English see Drake as a hero? What source could they use to support this view?
  c Can you think of any English people who might not see Drake as a hero?

2 **Facts** are things that we know to be true. **Points of view** are people's own ideas about things.

  Copy these sentences. Put **F** next to the ones that are facts. Put **P** next to the ones that are points of view.

  • *Drake lived at the time of Queen Elizabeth I.*

  • *Drake was a brave man.*

  • *Drake sailed around the world.*

  • *Drake was one of the privateers.*

9 Why did the Armada fail?

In the summer of 1588 Philip II of Spain sent 130 ships, the **Armada**, to attack England. The plan was to meet a Spanish army at Calais and take it across the Channel to invade England. Everyone expected the plan to work.

As soon as the Armada reached the Channel the English ships attacked. The Armada carried on up the Channel. It sailed at the speed of the slowest ship. The English kept on attacking, but they could not stop it. It took four days to reach Calais, but the Armada had only lost two ships when it got there.

While the Armada was at Calais the English set fire to eight of their old ships. They sailed these **fireships** into the middle of the Armada. The Spanish panicked. Many captains cut away their anchors to escape quickly. The English were waiting to attack. They damaged many Spanish ships with cannon fire. Then there was a storm. The Armada was split up. It could not keep together, or anchor, or meet the army now. So the Spanish decided to go home another way, around the tip of Scotland and Ireland. Only 40 ships got back to Spain in late September.

This picture was painted about twenty years after the Armada sailed. Many Spanish ships were high at the back. This made them hard to sail in a strong wind. Some of the Spanish crew were not sailors. They had not been trained to fire cannons quickly. Some English ships were much lower at the back. This made them easier to sail. The English crews were all well trained.

Source B

My health is bad and I know that I am always sea sick. The Armada is so big and so important that the person in charge should understand navigation and sea fighting, and I know nothing of either.

Part of a letter to King Philip II of Spain, from the man he chose to lead the Armada. Philip still chose him.

Activities

1 Read Source B. Did the man Philip chose want to lead the Armada? What were his reasons?

2 Look at Source A. Read the caption.
  a Trace the outline of a ship that is definitely Spanish.
  b Trace the outline of a ship that is definitely English.

This is a painting of the fireships at Calais. Fireships were old ships which were set on fire and sailed towards the enemy.

Source D

They have a captain for their ship, a captain for their guns and a captain for each group of soldiers. This leads to great confusion.

Written by a captain of one of the English ships which fought against the Armada.

Source E

Whenever we fired a cannon we had at least an hour's work to load it again.

Written by a sailor on a Spanish ship during a battle in 1589.

Source F

An English medal, made after the Armada was beaten. The words around the edge say 'God breathed, and they were scattered'. This is referring to the storm which damaged the Armada after it left Calais.

Why did things happen?

People argue over why the Armada failed. Here are some causes that they give. A **cause** is something that makes things happen.

- The ship **design** of both sides. The English ships could sail better.
- The **training** of both crews. The Spanish had not been trained to keep loading and firing cannons. The English had.
- Spanish **cannons** were long, heavy, difficult to re-load. English cannons were shorter and easier to move.
- The **fireships**. These caused the panic at Calais, and split up the Armada for the English to fire at.
- The **weather**. This was very bad. It affected both sides, but the English could shelter in English ports.

1 Copy this table and finish it. You have to find a source which tells you something about that cause. Make sure you always explain what the source tells you about the cause.

Cause	Source or sources which tell you about it
Design	Source A, it shows the Spanish ships were higher.

2 Think about all the work you have done, and everything you have read about the Armada. Why do you think the Armada failed?

Source G

Many of the enemy's ships were better than us in battle. Better designed, with better guns, gunners, and crew. If on the day we arrived at Calais the army had come we could have won.

Written by Don Francisco de Bobilla, commander of the soldiers on board the Armada.

10 Was Guy Fawkes framed?

On 5 November 1605 Guy Fawkes was caught trying to blow up King James I and Parliament. He was found in a cellar under the House of Lords. He was just about to set light to 36 barrels of gunpowder. Fawkes was arrested and tortured. He said there had been other people in the plot. A search was made for the rest of the plotters. Some were killed trying to escape. The rest were questioned, tried, and found guilty. They were hanged.

The government said they had found out about the plot when a Catholic lord was sent a letter telling him to stay away from Parliament. He gave the letter to **Robert Cecil**, James I's chief minister. Cecil told King James. They sent some soldiers to the cellar and caught Guy Fawkes. But there are some things about the story that make some people ask the question 'Was Guy Fawkes framed?'

Source A

It has pleased God to uncover a plot to kill the King, Queen, Prince and the most important men of this land by secretly putting much gunpowder into a cellar under Parliament, and blowing them all up at once.

Written by Robert Cecil to the English Ambassador in Brussels on 9 November 1605.

Source B

We cannot hope to run the country while many people obey foreign rulers. This is what Catholics do. The priests tell them that they must do everything to help their religion, even killing the King.

Robert Cecil is supposed to have said this.

Source C

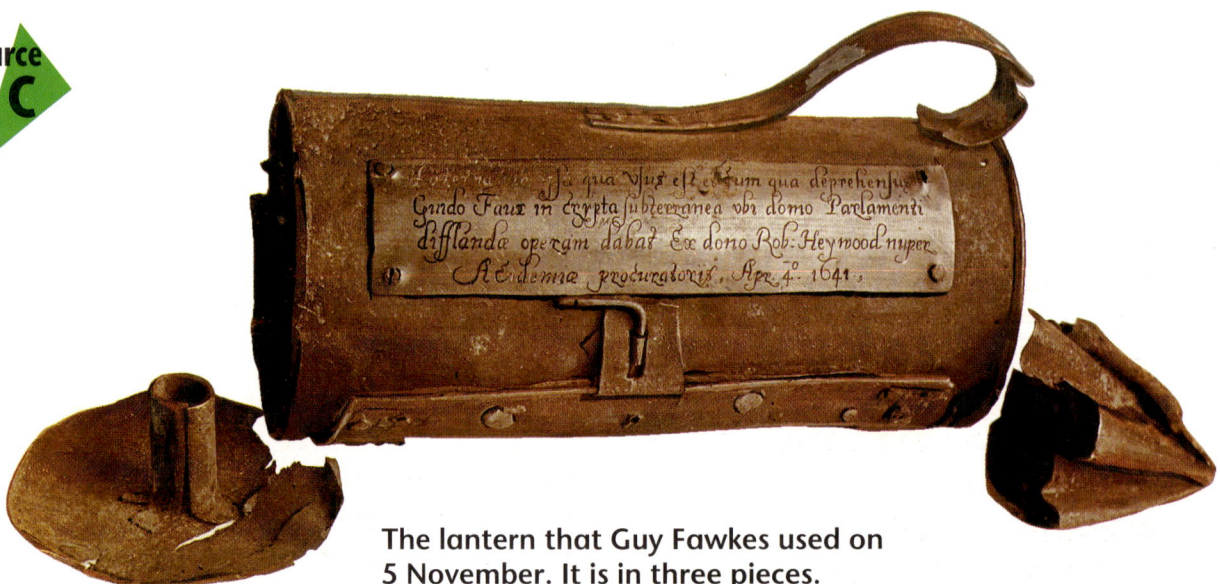

The lantern that Guy Fawkes used on 5 November. It is in three pieces. The brass label was added later.

DEO trin-vni Britanniæ bis ultori In memoriam Classis invincibilis subuerfæ submerfæ | Proditionis nefandæ detectæ difiectæ.
To God, In memorye of his double deliveraunce from yᵉ invincible Navie and yᵉ unmatcheable powder Treafon

Source D

This print was made just after the Gunpowder Plot. The Armada is out at sea to the left. The Pope and the Devil are plotting in the tent. The Pope was Head of the Catholic Church.

Source E

I hear that the Privy Council and some Lords were in Parliament and a barrel of gunpowder was lit under them. And that it went off, and most, if not all of them were blown up. I cannot believe so strange and desperate an act.

Written by a person living in Paris, to a friend in England in 1605.

Activities

1 Did you know the story of the Gunpowder Plot before now?
   a Which parts did you know before?
   b Which parts didn't you know?

2 Read Source A. If those people had been killed, how would this have affected the country?

3 What reason does Source D suggest for the Gunpowder Plot?

4 a Look at Source C. Imagine the lantern put together. Is it the same sort of lantern as the one in Source D?
   b If Source D has got the lantern right, does it have to be right about everything else it shows? Explain your answer.

5 Read Source E.
   a What did this person think had happened?
   b Imagine this person told you the story. Write a letter to another friend, telling the story.

This memorial to the Gunpowder Plot was painted in 1630. It shows God protecting the royal family, and punishing the plotters.

Source G

The Captain and I sat up late drinking and watching the boys in the street throwing fireworks. Today has been a holiday all through the City.

Written by Samuel Pepys in his diary on 5 November, 1661.

Source H

Those people who know how the government do things are sure that this is a trap, and that some members of the Privy Council have tricked these men.

Written by a Catholic visitor to England, in 1605.

Source I

Shocked by the Gunpowder Plot, the King and Parliament made laws against Catholics.

Written by a modern historian.

Source J

The usual story is that the plot really was discovered at the last minute. Others say it was a plot by Cecil to make James act against the Catholics. We can never know for sure.

A modern historian, writing about the Gunpowder Plot.

More information

Many people were worried that James I was not hard enough on the Catholics.

Robert Cecil was in charge of security. He could get into the Tower of London very easily.

Gunpowder was not something that you could just buy. All of the gunpowder in England was kept in the Tower of London.

Lists were kept of everything in the Tower of London. The lists for 1604 are missing.

How do we know?

1 Read Sources B and I.

Why might Cecil have wanted to frame Guy Fawkes?

2 Read Source G.
   a When was it written?
   b Why was 5 November a holiday?
   c How long had people been celebrating 5 November?
   d Which other source shows the same thing?

3 Would the list of what was in the Tower of London in 1604 help you to decide what happened? How would it help?

4 a Which source from the time says Fawkes and the others might have been framed?
   b Why should you be careful about believing this source?

5 a Do you think Guy Fawkes was framed? Explain your answer.
   b Can we know for sure?

11 How did people fight in the Civil War?

The Civil War began in 1642. The **Royalists** and the **Parliamentarians** fought each other over the way the country should be run. They had no modern weapons. They fought with pikes, muskets and cannons.

Pikes were very long spears. **Pikemen** always fought together in large groups, called **hedgehogs**.

Musketeers used a gun, called a musket. They carried gunpowder and a lighted fuse all the time. Muskets could kill from further away than pikes, but they took a long time to load and fire.

Pikemen and musketeers were called 'foot', because they fought together on foot. The other part of the army, the horsemen, were called 'horse'. The horsemen fought with pistols and swords.

Source A

A modern artist's idea of what a Civil War battle looked like.

Source B

Battles were confusing. It was hard to tell the sides apart because their clothes were similar. At the battle of Edgehill the sides used different coloured sashes to tell each other apart. Sir Faithful Fortescue's men changed sides. They forgot to take off their Parliamentarian sashes. Many of them were shot by the men they had just joined.

Written by a modern historian.

Source C

Pikes were between four to six metres long. Pikemen often cut down their pikes to make them easier to use. A pikeman had to be strong to use a pike, and to wear the heavy armour. He had a helmet and armour to cover his body, neck and thighs.

Written by a modern historian.

Activities

1 Find a pikeman in Source A. Is he like the description in Source C? Explain your answer.

2 a What does Source B say the sides used at the battle of Edgehill to tell each other apart?

b The armies also used passwords, which they chose before each battle. Read Source E, on page 52. What was the Royalist password at Edgehill?

c How might the Parliamentarians have found out what they Royalist password was?

All of the written sources on these pages are about the first real battle of the Civil War, at **Edgehill** in 1642. The battle started at midday and ended when it got too dark to fight. No one had won, the battle just stopped, and the soldiers moved on.

Source
D

From a stained glass window made soon after the Civil War, in memory of some of the soldiers who fought in it.

Source
E

We fired our cannons, and our horsemen charged. The enemy ran. We chased them for four miles. Many of them escaped by guessing our password, which was 'For God and King Charles'. The battle stopped when it grew dark. We killed many of their men. Even more have run away and will not come back.

Written by a Royalist horseman.

Source
F

Both armies began by firing their cannons. Our horseman charged theirs, and chased them for two to three miles. But the chase lost us the chance to win. Our horsemen did not come back to break up the enemy's foot soldiers. When the musketeers' ammunition was gone the pikemen fought. The King's flag was captured. We got it back at last, and the horsemen came back, but by then it was too late to fight any longer.

Written by a Royalist horseman.

Source
G

From a film about the Civil War, made in 1970.

They had more men than we expected. They had many horsemen. They had nine big groups of foot. After some cannon firing their horsemen charged us, and then the foot soldiers closed in. Our men were so fierce that the enemy musketeers hid behind their pikemen, rather than shoot at us. Many of the King's men ran away. Then it got dark. We had used all our ammunition, so we let them leave the battlefield.

Written by a Parliamentarian soldier.

We are tired out from keeping watch for so many nights. It was a long fight, too. It lasted from noon till dusk. No one was fed that night. I could not find my servant, who had my cloak. I had nothing to keep me warm, so I had to walk about all night. It was a cold night, with a sharp frost.

Written by a Parliamentarian soldier.

How do we know?

1 Look at Source D. Can you tell which side the soldiers were on?

2 a Look at Source G. What weapons can you see being used that were talked about in the text?

   b What weapon can you see being used that was talked about in the sources but not the text?

3 Which source do you think gives the best idea of what a battle was like? Explain your answer.

4 Which source do you think gives the best idea of what a soldier's life was like?

5 a Which of the sources would you use if you wanted to show that fighting in the Civil War was exciting? Why?

   b Which of the sources would you use if you wanted to show that being a soldier in the Civil War was uncomfortable? Why?

12 Life in Pepys' London

Charles I lost the Civil War. In 1649 he was executed. England was run by Parliament, and then by **Oliver Cromwell**. The government was Puritan. It passed laws to stop people doing things it thought were wrong. These included going to the theatre. Even Christmas celebrations were banned.

Many people still wanted a king at the head of the government. Soon after Oliver Cromwell died, Charles II came back to England. It was 1660. Many people celebrated the **restoration** (bringing back) of the Stuarts. They hoped to restore things to the way they had been before the Civil War.

But things were different, and they carried on changing. London had a bad outbreak of sickness (the plague), and a huge fire, which destroyed much of the city. Architects had to redesign parts of the city. The new St Paul's Cathedral was designed by Christopher Wren.

Source A

This is a picture of a part of London which was rebuilt after the Great Fire of 1666.

Source B

All the talk nowdays is that the King will come again. It seems to me that everybody wishes it. I hope it will be so.

Written by Samuel Pepys. He kept a diary from 1660–1669, which tells us a lot about life in London at this time.

Source C

The King has agreed to the conditions, and is to return. Great joy all yesterday in London. Bells were rung, bonfires lit and people drank the King's health.

Written by Samuel Pepys.

How did things change?

1 Look at Source C on page 15.
Write down:
- what the houses are made of
- what the shopfronts are like
- what the streets are like
- if there are any street lights
- what sort of transport there is
- the different types of people you can see.

2 Look at Source A. Make a list of the same things as in Question 1.
Put an **S** next to the things which are still the same. Put a **D** next to the things which are different.

3 Read the first two sentences of the text.
Now read Sources B and C.
Write a sentence about how people's feelings about kings seem to have changed between 1649 and 1660.

13 Plague!

The plague was spread by the fleas on rats biting people, putting the illness into their blood. People caught the plague all through Tudor and Stuart times. It was worse in the towns, where people were crowded together, and rats could live on the rubbish.

People did not know what caused plague, or how to stop it. All they knew was that it spread quickly, especially in hot weather, and that there was no known cure. One of the worst cases of the plague was the **Great Plague**, of 1665. It was very bad in London, where it killed over 100,000 people.

Symptoms of the plague

Temperature.
Headache.
Sickness.
Patient gets a lump (**buboe**) where the flea bite is.
The lump goes black.
Armpits, neck and legs get lumps.
Patient better after 10 days
OR
gets spots all over the skin, like bruises.
Patient dies.

Source B

22 July: There are not many people in London. I only met two coaches and two carts as I went home. Dr Burnett's servant died of a buboe and spots on his leg – that is the plague.

Written by Samuel Pepys, in 1665. He lived in London.

Source A

Dogs are killed. Great fires are made in the streets. People take medicines. None of this is sure to work.

Written in 1665 by William Petty, who was a scientist. He was writing about the plague.

Activities

1 Read Source A. Mr Petty says none of these things were sure to work.
Why did people do them?

2 Read the symptoms of the plague and Source B.
How did Pepys know that Dr Burnett's servant had the plague?

Source C

A modern artist's idea of the
plague carts collecting the dead.

Source D

A print made at the time of people burying plague bodies.

Source F

Searchers and doctors must check the sick and dead in each house for plague.

If there is plague in a house, the house, and the people in it, are shut up for a month after the last death there. The door of the house must be marked with a red cross and 'Lord Have Mercy Upon Us'.

Dead bodies must be buried two metres deep before sun-rise or after sun-set.

The streets must be kept clean. People are to be given the job of raking the rubbish away. Animals in the city are to be sent away or killed.

Government orders for London during the plague.

Source E

7 June: Today I saw two or three houses with a red cross on the doors, and 'Lord Have Mercy Upon Us'. A sad sight, they are the first I have seen. I bought some tobacco to smell and chew.
20 July: My Lady Carteret gave me a bottle of plague cure to take home with me.

Written by Samuel Pepys, in 1665.

Source G

7 September: I went to St James. It was sad and dangerous to see so many coffins in the streets. There are few people about, the shops are shut up, no one knows who will be next.

Written by John Evelyn, in 1665. He lived in London, like Pepys.

More information

Some people thought the plague was caused by bad air.

Some people thought it was caused by touching others.

Here are some things that people did to try to stop catching the plague:

- People lit bonfires in the streets to burn the bad air.
- People burnt herbs on the fire in sickrooms.
- People sucked tablets made of cinnamon and myrrh.
- People who had the plague had to stay at home. If they had no homes, they had to go to 'pest houses' where everyone had the plague.
- People would not go near houses where people had the plague.
- People burnt tar on the fire of the sickroom. This made a thick, black, bad smelling smoke.
- Money used in shops was put into bowls of vinegar, not passed from hand to hand.
- People drank sage, rue, buttercup, angelica roots and saffron mixed in sweet wine.

Source H

A plague doctor's outfit.

How do we know?

1 Read the information box.

  Make two lists:
  a A list of things people did that shows they thought the plague was in the air.
  b A list of things people did that shows they thought the plague was spread by touching other people.

2 What do you think the men in Source D think is a cause of the plague, air or touching? Explain your answer.

3 Which source would you use to show that some people had the right ideas?

4 Pepys was there. What did he think might help him avoid the plague?

14 Fire!

The Great Fire of London started on 2 September 1666, in Pudding Lane. Fires often happened in Tudor and Stuart times. Open fires were used for heating and cooking. Candles were used for lights. Accidents were likely with all these flames about. What was surprising about the Great Fire was how fast it spread, and how much of the city it burnt. Why was it such a bad fire?

To answer this question we have to look at the way that people fought fires at the time. We also need to look at how London was built. We are lucky to have the diary of Samuel Pepys, who was in London during the fire. He wrote down the things he saw and heard. This should give us some clues.

Source A

This is all that people had to fight the fire.

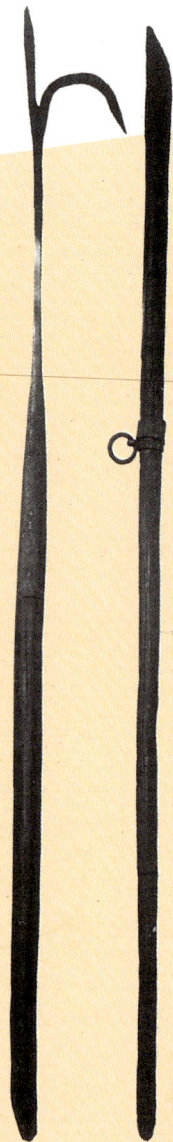

Source B

Jane woke us at three in the morning, to tell us of a great fire in the city. I went to her window. I thought it was far enough away and went back to bed. About seven I got up to dress, and looked out of the window. I saw the fire was dying out, and was further off.

Samuel Pepys writing in his diary on 2 September 1666.

Source C

Jane tells me that about 300 houses were burned down by the fire we saw. It is now burning down all of Fishstreet by London Bridge.

Samuel Pepys writing in his diary on 2 September 1666.

A modern artist's idea of what it was like during the fire.

A Dutch artist painted this picture of the fire at the time.

Source F

Nobody was trying to put it out. They were all trying to save their things and escape. The wind is driving the fire towards the City. After so long without rain, everything burns very easily, even the stone churches.

Written by Samuel Pepys on 2 September 1666.

Source H

The houses are very close together, and full of things that burn well, like tar and oil and brandy. The streets were full of people and horses and carts loaded with things, ready to run one another over, moving things from one burning house to another.

Written by Samuel Pepys on 2 September 1666.

Source G

I told the King what I saw, and he told me to tell the Lord Mayor to pull down the houses all around the fire. I met the Lord Mayor, who said: "What can I do? I am worn out! People will not obey me. I have been pulling down houses. But the fire is quicker than we are."

Written by Samuel Pepys on 2 September 1666.

Source I

With your face in the wind you were almost burned with a shower of firedrops. Houses five or six houses apart were set alight with these flakes of fire.

Written by Samuel Pepys on 3 September 1666.

Now begins the blowing up of houses in Tower Street, next to the Tower. It stopped the fire where it was done, bringing down the houses to the ground, and then it was easy to put out Going to the fire I found that by blowing up of houses, and the work of the workmen out of the shipyards, there is a good stop to it.

Written by Samuel Pepys on 4 September 1666.

Part of a map made soon after the fire which shows the buildings that survived.

Why did things happen?

1 Look at the picture sources.
Make a list of the reasons you think they show for the fire spreading so quickly.

2 Read the written sources.
Make a list of the reasons they give for the fire spreading so quickly.

3 Look at Source K. Read Source J.
   a What was the way of fire-fighting that stopped the fire?
   b When did the government start to use it?
   c Why do you think this is?

INDEX